REDISCOVERED

PERSONAL BOOKLET

Life

JOURNEYS

Copyright © CWR 2008
Published 2008 by CWR, Waverley Abbey House,
Waverley Lane, Farnham, Surrey GU9 8EP, UK.
Registered Charity No. 294387. Registered Limited
Company No. 1990308. Reprinted 2009.
Bible-reading notes included in this booklet previously
published by CWR in the January/February 2005 issue
of *Lucas on Life Every Day*, by Jeff Lucas and also in *Life
with Lucas Daily Readings Throughout the Year,* ISBN
978-1-85345-440-0, published by CWR, 2007.
The right of Jeff Lucas to be identified as the author of
this work has been asserted by him in accordance with
the Copyright, Designs and Patents Act 1988, sections
77 and 78.
Questions for group discussion: Jeff Lucas and Andy Peck
All rights reserved. No part of this publication
may be reproduced, stored in a retrieval system, or
transmitted, in any form or by any means, electronic,
mechanical, photocopying, recording or otherwise,
without the prior permission in writing of CWR.
For a list of our National Distributors visit
www.cwr.org.uk/distributors
Unless otherwise indicated, all Scripture references
are from the Holy Bible: New International
Version (NIV), copyright © 1973, 1978, 1984 by the
International Bible Society.
Concept development, editing, design and production
by CWR
Cover image: CWR
Printed in England by Bishops.
ISBN: 978-1-85345-466-0

DAILY READINGS: **JEFF LUCAS**
GROUP DISCUSSION QUESTIONS:
JEFF LUCAS AND ANDY PECK

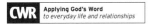

CWR Applying God's Word
to everyday life and relationships

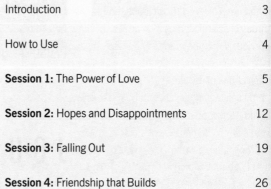

CONTENTS

INTRODUCTION

It had been a very difficult lunch, and I sensed the throes of seismic indigestion ahead. Even though I'd not previously met the man sitting across the table from me, he'd persistently pursued me. He was about to demand a huge chunk of my life.

'Jeff, I sense that you are lonely. You really need a best friend – and God has told me … I'm to be that friend. Here I am. When do we get started?'

My face flushed with panic. I was desperate to tell him that I already felt rich with vintage friendships that I was so very grateful for. That far from feeling lonely, I had the privilege of a great many significant friendships – so there wasn't a current need for a self-appointed best friend, or even a vacancy.

But instead I just sat and wondered at the bizarre way in which we Christians sometimes do life. Friendship is certainly one of the most valuable gifts we can enjoy. Without it, our days are walked in subdued black and white rather than in the warmth of colour. How priceless are those relationships that have long-term trust, easy laughter, and the comfortable sharing of silence as well as the delight of relaxed chatter. But relationships made of that stuff don't just drop out of the sky or get produced by announcement. It takes time, tears and, perhaps, a shared stroll through the autumnal lanes of tragedy to form something that begins to look like authentic friendship. Hence this *Life Journey*. May deeper, kingdom-centred friendships develop because we take this trek together.

How to use

This resource is
designed to include all
you will need for four
small-group sessions.
It comprises four DVD
clips, group discussion
questions based on
each clip and Bible
readings to be used
between each session.

PREPARATION

1. Watch the DVD clip before the meeting.

2. Use the icebreaker to get folk chatting. Select the
   questions that you think would be most useful for
   your group to look at. You may want to use them all,
   depending on the time you have available. We suggest
   you plan for 30–45 minutes.

THE SESSION

1. Play the DVD clip first and go straight into the
   icebreaker question.

2. Use the questions you have selected.

3. Move from discussion into prayer. There's a prayer
   included in the material which you could finish with at
   the end.

4. Encourage the group to use the daily readings in
   the days between sessions. The readings expand
   and build on the topics covered in the DVD. If the
   group members are not used to daily Bible reading,
   encourage them to develop this habit. If the group
   members are already into a routine of Bible reading
   and prayer each day you might want to discuss how
   best to work these new readings into their time.

5. You could start the next session by reviewing how the
   group found the daily readings. What did they learn?
   Do they have questions to raise? How did God speak?

Session 1:
The Power of Love

ICEBREAKER:
In today's society women have friends, while men just have people they do things with. Do you agree? Think of people you know – does this statement hold true?

FOR GROUP DISCUSSION:
- Was there a special childhood friendship you enjoyed? What made it so special?

- Think of your average week. How much time do you spend enjoying and cultivating friendship? Would you like the time spent to change?

- Think about your friends who are Christians and those who are not Christians. How do your friendships differ?

- What do you typically bring to a friendship (when you are being generous about yourself!)?

- What does it mean to journey with our friends when they go through tough times?

- What does a true friend look like?

- Have you ever tried to form a friendship, but found it didn't work? If so, what did you learn?

- In your group you may want to spend a little time praying briefly for individual friends who are currently going through challenging circumstances.

PRAYER:
Triune God,
You have never been alone.
You made us in Your image:
created to belong,
made for community,
called together.
Give us the gift of true friendship.
Deepen the relationships we enjoy
and grant that we might be thoughtful fellow travellers,
especially when times are difficult.
Amen.

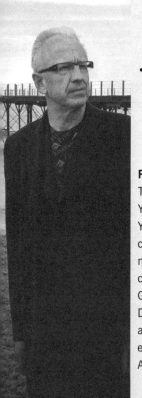

THE presence of an older brother would have been very helpful to me during my secondary school days. As a somewhat scrawny specimen (I was surely shortchanged when muscles were being distributed), I took my share of playground beatings. One memorable skirmish involved an inordinately large chap who sported Doc Marten boots the size of his head. Sadly, there was no big brother at my side to defend me, hence my casualty of a nose, which enables me to smell around corners.

But the predator Saul bumped into the 'older brother' of his traumatised Christian victims, a brother to surely be reckoned with: the risen, ascended Christ (Heb. 2:11–12).

On the Damascus road, as Jesus asked, 'Why are you persecuting *me?*' the terrified Saul suddenly realised that, as he had victimised helpless Christians, he had actually been taking a swing at God; not a good idea.

The key to understanding how to do relationships is to know that God is profoundly affected by the way that we act towards those around us. The way that we treat 'the least of His' is the way that we treat Him. So our relationships are part of our worship, which is about so much more than getting together at weekends to sing songs or affirm creeds. We move and affect the heart of God by the way that we treat people every day. When we choose to bless, we ultimately bless Him: and when we select the pathway of sniping unkindness, we take pot shots at Him too. Look again at that one you are tempted to hurt: they have a Brother standing next to them.

Prayer: Father, teach me this difficult lesson, that to serve another, is to serve You. Amen.

You did it to *me*

BIG PICTURE:
Acts 9:1–10
Matthew 25:31–40

FOCUS:
'I am Jesus, whom you are persecuting.'
(Acts 9:5)

God is profoundly affected by the way that we act towards those around us

Almost a casualty …

FOCUS:
'He tried to join the disciples, but they were all afraid of him …'
(Acts 9:26)

IMAGINE strolling into a new church for the first time – you'd surely hope for a warm, welcoming smile or a friendly handshake. Now consider what it would feel like if, as you nervously show your face, everyone starts screaming and freezes in abject terror – and all because *you* have shown up for church. That was Saul's experience when he first visited the church in Jerusalem. Their reaction is understandable when we remember Saul's notoriety as a fearsome opponent of Christ. Perhaps they feared that he was posing as a Christian – an 'undercover brother' – in order to infiltrate more effectively and then devastate the church family at Jerusalem. The door slammed in his face: they refused to allow him to join them.

Helpfully, Barnabas – a respected leader, a 'good man' (Acts 11:24), and possibly an old school pal of Saul (some commentators believe they studied together) was on hand and was willing to take a risk on the rejected Saul. He brokered a conciliatory meeting, and a most unusual addition was finally welcomed into their church. Of course, if Barnabas had not 'come alongside' Saul (his name, 'son of comfort', comes from the same word that describes the comforting ministry of the Holy Spirit), the Christian Church might have lost one of its greatest generals, a casualty of misunderstanding.

Sometimes we have to walk the pathway of risk that Barnabas took, as he tossed aside concerns for his reputation – and possibly his life. Believing the best of someone when the rest of the world believes the worst may be the first step towards releasing incredible potential in others. Taken any risks lately?

Taken any risks lately?

Prayer: Lord, show me someone today who needs another to come alongside them. Let me be that person. Amen.

8

BARNABAS had a proven track record when it came to discernment. He had the insight to determine that Saul was the genuine article some years earlier. Now he is sent as an ambassador of the church in Jerusalem to investigate a blossoming revival in Antioch, some three hundred miles north. Once again, his spiritual antenna is functioning accurately, as he 'saw the evidence of the grace of God'. Barnabas chose not to worry about some fairly significant details – such as whether these new believers should be circumcised or baptised – those issues would be sorted out later. What thrilled him was that he saw grace at work and that was enough to make him glad.

Relationships often fail because we are driven by a desire to have everything ordered in others' lives precisely as we would like it. We want them to worship using our style, our musical preferences, and study the version of the Bible that is our chosen translation. It would be even more helpful if they would adopt our theological view of the second coming, reach out to others using our 'proven' evangelistic methods, and enjoy the same preachers and teachers as us, too. It's simpler when everyone believes exactly the same thing about everything: it's just that this usually only happens in dangerous cults.

Let's resist the temptation to try to make others in our own image: that's already been done, by the One who alone was qualified to do it – God Himself, and we are *His* workmanship, His unique poetry (Eph. 2:10). Magnanimous heart that Barnabas had, he was big enough to spot God at work – and cheer. Let's look for grace – not clones.

Big-hearted Barnabas

BIG PICTURE:
Acts 11:19–26a
Ephesians 2:1–10

FOCUS:
'When he arrived and saw the evidence of the grace of God, he was glad …' (Acts 11:23)

Prayer: Lord, help me to see grace, and be gracious. Amen.

Barnabas hunts for Saul

BIG PICTURE:
Acts 11:26b
Colossians 3:12–17

FOCUS:
'Therefore, as God's chosen people, holy and dearly loved, clothe yourselves with compassion, kindness, humility, gentleness and patience.' (Col. 3:12)

Grace means

that ... you often

don't get what

you deserve

I ONCE saw a bumper sticker that saddened me: 'Don't get mad, get even.' A popular slogan, but one that speaks of an obsessive hunger for vengeance that erodes friendships, demolishes marriages and leave us all wondering what the next international calamity might be. If getting even is our primary motivation, it won't be long before our most prized relationships are shattered.

It was surely a 'grace irony' that Barnabas asked Saul to co-lead the thriving congregation in Antioch. This was a church that had been formed in the first place because of Stephen's death – which included Saul's campaign of violence against the church some eight years earlier. Christians had been scattered from Jerusalem, and they gossiped the gospel as they went; hence the move of God in Antioch. Now, bizarrely, Saul is called to minister to that which has partly come about as a result of his pre-Christian activities.

For any minister or leader, relocating to take up a new ministry position can be a nerve-racking time. But as Saul travelled to Antioch, a million thoughts must have raced through his mind. Some members of the flock there had their lives utterly disrupted because of his zeal: some had perhaps lost family members because of his killing spree. Could they possibly accept him as a leader? Would he walk into a solid wall of resentment?

Apparently, he had nothing to fear, as the church family at Antioch welcomed both Barnabas and Saul with open arms. No mention is made of any teething pains or conflict.

Grace means that, in relationships, you often don't get what you deserve. Don't get even. Forgive.

Prayer: Teach me, Father, to be kind and compassionate; forgiving, just as in Christ You forgave me. Amen

SAUL is at the crossroads of his ministry and, after years of playing supporting actor to Barnabas, he now steps into the spotlight as the leading player.

The relational tables are turning. Barnabas had taken the young convert Saul under his wing, Barnabas had opened the door for service for him in Antioch. But now it's Saul who takes the initiative and puts the scheming Elymas in the darkness of judgment. It's Saul who gets a name change and steps out of the chrysalis of training to become Paul, apostle to the Gentiles. And from now on, notice that Doctor Luke generally writes about *Paul and Barnabas*, rather than *Barnabas and Saul*. Like Andrew, who opened the door for his brother Peter to meet Jesus and then found himself standing in the shadows, so Barnabas now begins to take a secondary role. But a true friend is not only able to commiserate with us when things go wrong (which is easy, because we are in the place of strength) but is one who can authentically celebrate with us when things go very right, and we enjoy heady success and even prominence.

Paul would have his fair share of people who were envious of his ministry (Phil. 1:15) – but Barnabas certainly wasn't one of them. Paul would be able to write about love that 'does not envy' (1 Cor. 13:4), and Barnabas modelled that quality as Paul took the reins of being the key leader.

Jealousy has spoiled many a great friendship. As James writes, 'For where you have envy and selfish ambition, there you find disorder and every evil practice' (James 3:16).

Prayer: Father, keep jealousy out of my heart and mind today. Amen.

Learning to play second fiddle

BIG PICTURE:
Acts 13:3–12
Philippians 1:15–18
James 3:16

FOCUS:
'Then Saul, who was also called Paul …'
(Acts 13:9)

Session 2:
Hopes and disappointments

ICEBREAKER:
Write down the names of your five closest friends.
How long have you known them: 0–2 yrs; 2–5 yrs;
5–10 yrs; 10+ yrs ? Where did you meet? (eg school/uni,
church, work, leisure, other)
Do you think this exercise tells you anything about your
ability to make friends through life?

FOR GROUP DISCUSSION:

- How can we 'invest' in our friendships?

- Do we tend to give people 'space to grow' or do we tend
  to tag our friends according to their weaknesses?

- Do you have friends that, in hindsight, you are surprised
  to be close to?

- One study suggests that if you have five good friends in
  a church you are unlikely to leave, however unpleasant
  things get. Do you agree?

- Think of your friends. Are they similar (eg age, ethnic
  background, education, sex)? Is there a category of
  person that you would find it hard to imagine having a
  friendship with?

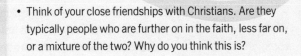

- Think of your close friendships with Christians. Are they typically people who are further on in the faith, less far on, or a mixture of the two? Why do you think this is?

- Many Christians have friendly relations with people in the church they serve with, although they would never call them 'friends' since they never become close. Do you think that this matters?

- How do we maintain the unity of the Spirit practically?

- What role can a third party have in resolving a relationship problem? Can you think of passages of Scripture to help you?

Prayer:
Father,
teach us to build true friendship.
Help us to bring repair
where there is damage
and give us wisdom to navigate
through times of conflict.
May the unity
You have given as a gift
be cherished
and maintained.
Amen.

Beloved Luke
and others:
still here

BIG PICTURE:
Colossians 4:14
Philemon 24
2 Timothy 4:10

FOCUS:
'Demas, because he
loved this world, has
deserted me ...'
(2 Tim. 4:10)

I AM blessed to know some people – a few – who are truly vintage friends; they have believed in me when no one else did, prayed me through my storms and cheered me on in the rain. Sometimes we struggle to think of something specifically to be thankful for in a friendship; but Paul was grateful for friends just because they were still there, still walking with him after many years. There is a measure of sadness in his words to the Colossians as he mentions 'Dear Luke the doctor', and then in the same breath, without any words of affection, 'Demas'. It's clear that Demas dropped out of the battle of faith, leaving the ranks of Paul's friends and fellow soldiers.

But Luke, who some believe was Paul's personal physician, stood firmly with Paul not only in his earlier imprisonment but also through later trials, by which time Demas had deserted him (2 Tim. 4:10). Of course Luke is the author of the third Gospel and of Acts (cf. Acts 1:1). And there were others singled out by Paul as being 'dear' to him – and most of those who are dear are also described as faithful.

Those who have been our friends for years have seen us at our best and at our worst. They have observed us at an intimate level. They know when we are struggling, and are privy to some of the sins that we fight. Despite all this, they are still willing to be numbered as our friends. Be grateful, and count them as dear: they are still around.

Prayer: Father, thank You for those who know the real truth about me, but love me anyway. Bless them today. Amen.

THERE are some people who relish every opportunity to correct others – and often they are clumsy as they do so. Others seem to have a very genuine gift of lovingly coming alongside us, bringing gentle correction that inspires rather than damages. Two of Paul's closer friends, Aquila and his wife Priscilla, were made of such stuff. Paul did not surround himself with 'yes people'.

They met Paul first in Corinth; sharing his profession as leather workers, they invited him into their home, where he stayed for around 18 months. They became very close helpers to Paul. Although we don't have any details, they literally put their lives on the line for him (Rom. 16:3–4).

But the help that they gave to a young visiting preacher, Apollos, shows their ability to speak plainly but lovingly. Apollos had huge gaps in his theology (only teaching John's baptism), but was extremely gifted and later became very popular (1 Cor. 1:12; 3:4). This gracious couple took him into their home in Ephesus (not embarrassing him in public) and gave him the fuller story of the life and work of Jesus.

Our relationships should include the possibility of straight talk, but proceed with care. Do we find that we rather enjoy the feeling that we get when correcting others? Have those that we rush to rebuke ever actually given us permission to speak into their lives? The fact that we are Christians certainly does not give us an 'access all areas' pass to other people's lives, simply because they are Christians too. Are we willing to be corrected ourselves, or are we deluded into believing that we have graduated from that need?

Prayer: Father, deliver me from rushing to correct others, and resisting correction myself. Amen.

An honest but kind couple

BIG PICTURE:
Acts 18:1–28
1 Corinthians 16:19
2 Timothy 4:19

FOCUS:
'When Priscilla and Aquila heard him, they invited him to their home and explained to him the way of God more adequately.'
(Acts 18:26)

Are we willing to be corrected ourselves?

Titus and those Cretans

BIG PICTURE:
Titus 1:1–16

FOCUS:
'Cretans are always liars, evil brutes, lazy gluttons.' (Titus 1:12)

WE KNOW that Paul sometimes used words that seem inflammatory and harsh. John Mark was dubbed 'apostate', the 'circumcision group' in the Galatian churches were told to go ahead and castrate themselves (Gal. 5:12) and here Paul engages in what seems to be, at least, some blatant racial stereotyping – and at worst, outright racial prejudice. He writes to Titus, a leader on special assignment, 'our man in Crete'.

Paul explodes with the outrageous smear, 'Cretans are always liars', perhaps because he felt such affection for Titus and was defending him. Titus was one of only three men that Paul referred to as 'his son' – the others being Timothy and Onesimus (2 Tim. 1:2; Philem. 10). Prejudice is a subtle virus: it may linger deep within and almost go unnoticed until the right difficulty ignites it, with ugly results. Some commentators rush to defend Paul, saying that he was only quoting a popular philosopher's words – but he definitely seems to endorse them! While it's true that culture was very different then, let's also remember that Paul was not infallible. Because he said it, doesn't make it right.

And using the phrase 'you always' is usually guaranteed to be unhelpful. It is rarely true (children aren't always untidy, even if some of them manage a 99% success rate; there are moments when their bedrooms are clean). It's a demotivating phrase too: if our friends and family members think, when we use that 'always' word, that this is the perception that we have of them, what point is there in them behaving any differently? Avoid making generalisations – they are nearly always rooted in prejudice.

Prejudice is a subtle virus …

Prayer: Father, root out all prejudice from my heart. Help me to avoid stereotyping others, or focusing on their faults. Amen.

THE New Testament is loaded with people – at least seventy – who are only named there because of their friendship with Paul, who 'attracted friends around him as a magnet attracts iron filings', according to F. F. Bruce. Some we know very little about, except that Paul loved them dearly. In his epistles, he uses the words 'brother', 'brotherly', 'brothers' and 'brethren' a total of 136 times (ladies please note – the words he uses refer to both male and female!) Paul celebrated his dearest friends with words of great tenderness. Friendship mattered to him greatly, and his letters reveal that he felt the pain of separation keenly and that he thought often about the lives of those he loved. He did not see those friends merely in terms of what they could do for him, but genuinely paid great interest in them and in their hopes and dreams.

We skip over most of the names when we are reading Scripture – and perhaps miss the fact that Paul recorded them because they were so valued by him. Some profoundly disappointed him; some were a special delight: '… Urbanus, our fellow worker in Christ … my dear friend Stachys … Rufus, chosen in the Lord, and his mother, who has been a mother to me, too' (Rom. 16:9,13).

Who would make our 'list of seventy'? Who are the people that have impacted us? Paul let his friends know, loud and clear, that they were important to him: he was very willing to express his love freely, without hesitation. We should go out of our way – before offering a tribute at a funeral – to do the same.

Delights and disappointments

BIG PICTURE:
Romans 16:1–27

FOCUS:
'Greet Ampliatus, whom
I love in the Lord.'
(Rom. 16:8)

Prayer: Father, may I genuinely value, appreciate and celebrate my close friendships – and find the words to express how much they mean to me. Amen.

Alexander: let God be judge

BIG PICTURE:
Romans 12:9–21
2 Timothy 4:14

FOCUS:
'... leave room for God's wrath.' (Rom. 12:19)

WE DON'T know exactly what the infamous Alexander did to Paul – but we do know that he hurt Paul very badly. 'He did me *a great deal of harm*', says the apostle; the words used literally mean 'to display information' and suggests that Alexander was an informer who testified falsely against Paul before a Roman magistrate. Perhaps the metal worker turned against his former friend and sought to ruin him.

At first, it seems like Paul is using some inflammatory language again: 'The Lord will repay him for what he has done.' It sounds like one of those 'Break the teeth of my enemies, God' imprecatory prayers that we find in the Psalms. But look again, because Paul is not saying 'I'll repay that traitor all right – I'll get him', but rather is leaving his cause with God and allowing the justice of God to operate. Paul amplifies this idea in Romans 12:9 as he insists that we 'leave room for God's wrath'. Forgiving someone who has hurt us is not suggesting we reject the possibility of justice – rather we hand the situation to the One who will always do justly – and leave it to Him.

One thing that would surely disqualify a judge from operating in any court of law is the suspicion of bias. There are some situations where we have been so wounded, that we need to allow the One who will surely do right (Psa. 9:8) to deliver a ruling – we cannot possibly deliver a fair verdict in those particular proceedings.

Prayer: Lord, show me where I am still trying to be judge and jury, instead of resting in Your loving justice. Amen.

... hand the

situation to

the One who

will always

do justly ...

18

Session 3:
Falling out

ICEBREAKER:
Can you think of a situation that makes you especially sad, where friends have fallen out? This could either be in your life or one you have read about in the media.

FOR GROUP DISCUSSION:
- Some friendships explode – and others erode. What usually happens when someone disagrees with you? How good are you at having a difference of opinion with someone?

- Are there issues where a difference of opinion will always lead to a relationship breakdown, or should we be able to agree to differ regardless?

- Think of a time when you were tempted to break up with a friend. Why did you not do so? How did the situation become resolved?

- Think of friends to whom you are no longer close. What would it take to resume a relationship?

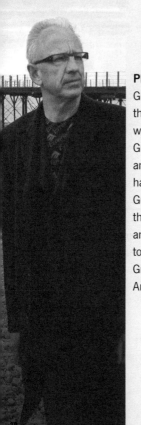

- Have you ever been involved in a 'gift war' – what happened?

- How would you be most likely to irritate those who are close to you, and how are you most likely to be irritated?

PRAYER:
Guard our hearts, Lord,
that seeds of bitterness
will find no place there.
Guard our lips, Lord,
and save us from speaking
hasty and unkind words.
Guard our gifts
that we might cooperate together
and never allow what's so important to us
to become a reason for division.
Grant us veteran friendships.
Amen.

THE strongest relationships can be destroyed by the presence of long-term resentment. Today we see perhaps the beginning of the end for the mighty coalition between Paul and Barnabas. Paul is very much at the helm of the little missionary team now, and he takes the wheel with a firm grip – not without some relational fallout. John Mark, Barnabas' cousin and assistant to Barnabas and Saul back in Antioch, decides that he wants to abandon the journey mid-trip. Luke doesn't tell us why the sudden change of heart happened – perhaps as a relative of Barnabas, John Mark resented Paul for suddenly taking the lead. He may have been scared about the perils ahead (2 Cor. 11:26), or even seriously ill. But, for whatever reason, he quit, which the trailblazing Paul saw as tantamount to desertion of his post. Paul would later refuse to give him a second chance, rejecting him from the team (Acts 15:39), and drafting in Timothy to fill the gap. Sometimes aggressive visionaries aren't the easiest people to get along with: strong on faith, but short on compassion.

Press the pause button for a moment. Something considerable has happened here, a relatively small fracas that will grow into the total breakdown between Paul and Barnabas. Did resentment begin its slow, erosive work here?

Perhaps Barnabas was biased in later siding with his young cousin but the fact is, whoever was right or wrong, this issue was destined to cause the unravelling of a union that God had ordained. Let's deal quickly with misunderstandings – before they produce long-term destruction.

Prayer: Father, give me bravery to deal with conflict and misunderstanding, before resentment takes its toll. Amen.

SESSION 3: DAY 1

Seeds of division between the great friends

BIG PICTURE:
Acts 13:13–15
2 Timothy 4:11
Colossians 4:10–11
Ephesians 4:31–32

FOCUS:
'Get rid of all bitterness ...'
(Eph. 4:31)

The strongest relationships can be destroyed by the presence of long-term resentment

Dancing in the dark

BIG PICTURE:
Acts 13:42–52
2 Corinthians 7:6–7

FOCUS:
'God, who comforts the downcast, comforted us by the coming of Titus ...' (2 Cor. 7:6)

RELATIONSHIPS can be complex and demanding, so there are times when we're tempted to think – why bother? Today, as we see the strange sight of Paul and Barnabas driven out of town by jealousy, we get a glimpse of one of the great benefits of true friendship – the ability to laugh in the face of difficulty, rejection and pain.

The pair had been having a little too much success. So some political shenanigans took place among the key movers and shakers of the city, and the next thing – the two are expelled.

But we don't see them throwing a pity party. They seem to enjoy the whole thing, almost thumbing their noses at the city. They shake the dust off their sandals, an act that said 'even the dirt around here is defiling, and we don't want it between our toes, thank you' … and they are 'filled with joy'.

It's not that either one of them was incapable of sadness. Paul wrote about his blue period to the Corinthians, where he had 'despaired even of life' (2 Cor. 1:8–9). But friendship enables us to laugh when we are tempted to cry, as we share the burden, seeing problems in true perspective rather than being dwarfed by them. We won't all be kicked out of cities for Jesus, but we know that life on planet Earth will afford us our fair quota of pain, tears and some rejection here and there. The presence of a true friend can make all the difference at those times. Paul prized those friends who stood with him in the darkest times, like Onesiphorus and Titus (2 Cor. 7:6–7; 2 Tim. 1:16).

The presence of a true friend can make all the difference

Prayer: Lord, You are 'the God who gives endurance and encouragement'. Use me to bring both to others today. Amen.

I LOOKED into the eyes of an older Christian leader recently, and saw that, where hope had once been, now there was only rejection and pain. For a variety of reasons, many of those he has worked with in ministry for years no longer want to be with him.

Sometimes those who have been the very closest of friends part for good. For Paul, a terrible argument with Barnabas brought their God-ordained working partnership to an end. These men had known each other intimately for years, trekking hundreds of miles of dusty roads, sharing a thousand conversations. But they had a 'sharp dispute' over team selection for the next missionary journey – and reached a total impasse. The Greek text paints a portrait of two men in solidly fixed opinions, neither willing to give way to the other at all.

So, was it all for the best anyway, making Paul more effective in the new partnerships that would emerge with Timothy and Silas? Some commentators would have us think so, but I wonder if that's because we don't want our heroes to be too flawed. The notion that Paul may have been hard-hearted and hot headed – or that Barnabas was inappropriately protective of his young cousin – makes us feel uncomfortable. But the fact is, God *had* called these two together: did immaturity shatter what the Lord intended for further effectiveness? It's likely that the two remained distant friends, but their ministry together was over, even though the issue that divided them was relatively small. Too many great partnerships never reach their full potential. Are you wilfully damaging a relationship? Why not stop now, before it's too late?

Prayer: Lord, help me to invest in, value and honour those I have walked with for years, and never take them for granted. Amen.

The end of an era

BIG PICTURE:
Acts 15:36–41
Ephesians 4:25–32

FOCUS:
'Be kind and compassionate to one another, forgiving each other, just as in Christ God forgave you.'
(Eph. 4:32)

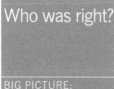

Who was right?

BIG PICTURE:
Acts 15:40–41
1 Corinthians 3:1–4

FOCUS:
'You are still worldly. For since there is jealousy and quarrelling among you, are you not worldly? Are you not acting like mere men?' (1 Cor. 3:3)

SO WHO was right in the terrible argument about poor John Mark? Even though the church at the time seemed to side with Paul, going out of their way to 'commend' his new partnership with Silas (the same verb was used about Paul and Barnabas on their return from their first tour in Acts 14:26) the truth is, we really don't know who was correct. Was either one right or wrong?

Supporters of Barnabas will be glad to know that John Mark actually did end up doing well – he sailed off to Cyprus, served with Peter (1 Pet. 5:13) and finally – ironically – served alongside Paul himself (Col. 4:10; 2 Tim. 4:11). Was Paul therefore guilty of prejudging the situation? Was the gentle encourager vindicated by later events?

Paul's fans would note that Barnabas did have a tendency sometimes to be more led by his heart than his head, as in the conflict over how to treat Gentile converts (Gal. 2:13). And the new partnerships with Silas and Timothy were successful.

But the reality is that no one emerges from this conflict completely vindicated – a lesson we would do well to learn in our own relationships and in church life. Our compulsion to be proven to be right often makes us declare in haste that even God Himself is on our side, as chief endorser of our opinion, our chosen style, our preferred taste. Let's not seek to be seen as right, but rather be those who seek the bigger picture, that of a peaceful way forward in conflict. 'Told you so' doesn't sound right coming from the lips of Christians.

Prayer: Father, please correct when I'm wrong, and keep me gracious and humble when I'm right. Amen.

Let's not seek

to be seen

as right ...

CONFLICT is not usually calm and measured. As we spar and jab back and forth in the heat of the moment, hurt and anger fuel our words like petrol on a bonfire. Before long, we've said things that we never meant to say, but it's too late: the damage has been done.

Paul certainly was guilty of using some heavy language in his skirmish with Barnabas. The Greek text reveals that he used a word linked with apostasy to describe John Mark's decision to turn back from the first missionary journey. Whatever John Mark did, he was surely not an apostate, and he was still willing to serve the Lord faithfully. Scared he may have been, but he was not guilty as charged. No wonder Barnabas rushed to defend his relative in the face of Paul's accusations.

Words can cut like a knife – and that's particularly true if you are articulate. My primary gift is that of communication and public speaking – and so I hope that I can craft words that will bless and inspire, but I confess with shame that the opposite is also true. I have to be very careful if I get into an argument, because, sadly, I have been guilty of putting together a few sentences or phrases that sliced like a razor blade: my gifting thus is hijacked and used to damage and bruise rather than bless.

We'd all do well to be those who are 'slow to speak' – who consider the long-term damage that we might be doing to our relationships before we rush to open our mouths and say things that we will live to regret.

Prayer: Father, help me to think before I speak today. Let my words come from response rather than reaction. Amen.

Warning – explosive words kill friendships

BIG PICTURE:
Galatians 5:13–15
James 4:11–12

FOCUS:
'Do not slander one another.' (James 4:11)

Session 4:
Friendship that builds

ICEBREAKER:

Describe your perfect day with a friend (or a combination of friends or different friends at different times of the day). Money and distance – no object. If you wish, you can breakfast in Paris and lunch in Rio.

FOR GROUP DISCUSSION:

- Can you think of a time when a friend said something to you to help or correct you – which, although you found it painful at the time, was ultimately helpful?

- Do you often 'correct' friends when you know they are out of line? How do you go about it so that they can receive it – or what stops you?

- How much is your behaviour actually shaped by close friends? Can you think of things you do now which a friend has modelled or suggested to you?

- When asked, in a survey, how they grow in discipleship, the majority of people said that they learned more from what was modelled by friends than through sermons or Bible study. Would this be true for you? Should we abandon the sermon?

- Do you tend to want your friends to be like you? If so, why?

- 'People are God's people' – what does it mean to 'respect' our friends?

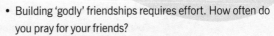

- Building 'godly' friendships requires effort. How often do you pray for your friends?
  a) Regularly, using a list or aide memoire;
  b) Only when they ask me specifically;
  c) Once in a blue moon;
  d) If I am honest, never.

- Have you ever felt 'out of the loop' and excluded because you were not friends with the 'in crowd'? Is it inevitable that this will happen? Or should we always work on being inclusive?

- Are you investing in a 'mentoring' friendship with someone?

PRAYER:
Father,
give us strong, healthy friendships
where we can challenge, comfort,
strengthen and confront each other.
Help us to give permission to others
to help us to grow.
Grant that our friendships
be naturally centred around You and Your purposes.
As we grow closer together,
save us from exclusivity.
Make us, we pray,
truly Your family together.
Amen.

People of wisdom needed

BIG PICTURE:
1 Timothy 1:1–2
Titus 2:1–8

FOCUS:
'Timothy, my true son in the faith.' (1 Tim. 1:2)

AS A preacher, I have spoken millions of words in public – and there are quite a few that I wish had never been spoken. That's certainly true when I consider how, years ago, I used to reflect about my very first preaching experience. The sermon, I would say, was truly hideous – but of course, it didn't matter, because 'There were only three old ladies and a dead cat in the congregation that heard it'. People would laugh at the line: now, I almost cry when I think that I was foolish enough to say it.

That throwaway line, though never intended to be hurtful, was in fact utterly demeaning and disrespectful to elderly people. How many of them winced when I likened them to a dead animal; how many, who already felt marginalised in what is all too often a young person's world, felt even more surplus to requirements as I unwittingly derided them?

We need to celebrate and honour our seniors, and not just out of some patronising sense of duty, but because many of them are possessors of a priceless treasure: wisdom. They got it, not from books, but from walking through the sun and the shadows of life. The Bible makes it clear that they can be vital fathers and mothers in the faith. Timothy was certainly Paul's number one son: no one is dubbed 'my son' by the apostle more; 'I have no one else like him' (Phil. 2:20), Paul affirms. If you're young, then treasure those seniors; and if you're older, consider this: are there a few spiritual juniors around you who know you as mum or dad?

Prayer: Father, bless and encourage those who sometimes feel so unneeded. Raise up more spiritual parents. Amen.

THE man concerned was an extremely strong leader, and was renowned for his skills in helping to disciple younger believers. But I was troubled, noticing that they began to talk like him, laugh at what he was amused at, and even enjoy the music he preferred. They were becoming copies of him.

Similarly, parents can be tempted to live out their dreams through their children. When their own aspirations are frustrated, they then try to realise them through their offspring – often with disastrous results. A new Christian, like a child, is very vulnerable and pliable. The saying 'Children are wet cement' applies to those young in faith too. All of which means that we need to be especially careful to avoid passing on our preferences, prejudices, ministry and calling to others. Making disciples is not about producing clones of ourselves but prompting and helping people to be made into the likeness of Christ.

Paul did invite people to imitate him – but only as he imitated Christ. He never seeks to make Timothy into a miniature version of himself. Rather, he is very aware of the specific prophetic calling that was upon the younger man's life, and only wants to instruct him 'in keeping with the prophecies once made about [him]' (1 Tim. 1:18). Apparently, when Timothy was commissioned, various predictions and promises were given to him. Paul sought only to nudge his true son further along the tracks of destiny laid out by God. Don't rush to be the voice that redirects other people's lives; rather, seek to find out what the Lord has already said to them, and help them walk that pathway.

Prayer: Lord, help me to be a part of Your ongoing work in the lives of others, and not a distraction to Your purposes. Amen.

No copies needed

BIG PICTURE:
1 Timothy 1:18–2:15

FOCUS:
'Timothy, my son, I give you this instruction in keeping with the prophecies once made about you, so that by following them you may fight the good fight.'
(1 Tim. 1:18)

Making disciples is … helping people to be made into the likeness of Christ

Lighten up

BIG PICTURE:
1 Timothy 3:1–4:16

FOCUS:
'For everything God
created is good, and
nothing is to be rejected
if it is received with
thanksgiving.'
(1 Tim. 4:4)

WHEN I first became a Christian, I was a frowning
zealot, white hot with spiritual passion – but was often
profoundly unhappy as well, because I was so very
intense about my Christian life. Surely, one might think,
it's impossible to be too intense about the things of God.
I disagree. I was so determined to do the right thing that I
became nervous about participating in some of the very
wonderful blessings that God wanted me to enjoy. Many
new believers fall into the trap of mistaking unhealthy
intensity with godly passion. And it seems that the Early
Church – and perhaps Timothy himself – was prone to this
kind of extreme zeal, rejecting some wonderful elements
of life as being profane – like the joys of marriage and
eating certain foods. Paul is saying – 'Go ahead, enjoy
God's lavish provision – celebrate and be thankful!'

The temptation for the committed is to either be lax
about their behaviour – or go to the other extreme and be
neurotic. The Pharisees fell into this trap, condemning
Jesus' party-going – and by pointing the finger at the
perfect Son of God, they were trying to be more 'holy'
than God Himself.

We tend quickly to applaud zeal – but let's help people
to know that it is actually possible to be unwise in our
passion, and go beyond where God asks us to go. The
new Christian who 'just has' to pray for three hours a day
and feels guilty about everything may not be a budding
intercessor with a tender heart: they may have brought
their pre-Christian personality traits into their spiritual life.

**Prayer: Father, save me and others from zeal without
wisdom. Help me to enjoy Your good gifts today.
Amen.**

ONE of the more delightful elements I discovered when I preached in the Caribbean Cayman Islands was a refreshing culture of respect. *Mr* Smith was going to read Scripture, not just 'Fred'. I'm not into titles, but everyone insisted on calling me 'Reverend Jeff'– and the children even tagged me as 'Mr Jeff'. I felt as though I had stepped back 50 years, into a kinder, more genteel age. It felt good.

Without sounding too much like 'disgusted' of Tunbridge Wells, I notice that one of the casualties of twenty-first-century living in Britain is respect. The art of having good manners seems to have fallen into neglect. Do you notice the dearth of such courtesies as 'please' or 'thank you', men's inability to be respectful to women (sacrificed on the altar of political correctness), the fact that nothing seems sacred any more, or the ease with which so many seem to slide into very bad language? Paul reminds Timothy to treat others with dignity (1 Tim. 5:1–4) – but then addresses the younger man with gracious respect too, calling him 'man of God' (1 Tim. 6:11).

Sometimes our very closest relationships can be damaged because familiarity breeds contempt, and we take people for granted. Remember that your son or daughter is also your brother or sister in Christ – and give them the same deference that you give to that person whom you see once a week at church. Leaders, be reminded that there is no such thing as pew fodder: people are not foot soldiers in a faceless army. Treat people with dignity, and many will live more dignified lives.

Prayer: Lord, never let my closeness to people lead me to disrespect or rudeness. Let my words be gracious, building others in faith. Amen.

Dignity and respect

BIG PICTURE:
1 Timothy 5:1–6:21

FOCUS:
'Do not rebuke an older man harshly, but exhort him as if he were your father.' (1 Tim. 5:1)

Treat people with dignity, and many will live more dignified lives

Remembering and praying

BIG PICTURE:
2 Timothy 1:3;
4:9–12

FOCUS:
'... night and day I constantly remember you in my prayers.'
(2 Tim. 1:3)

'I'LL pray for you.' I've said those words many times – and sometimes I forget to follow through and actually pray. For Paul, thinking regularly about his friends and 'remembering' them was very connected to his practice of praying for them frequently. Five times in his letters Paul speaks about remembering and praying. He saw this not as some kind of duty but as a delightful privilege. In fact, praying for our friends can be a real source of joy to us, even as we pray, as we recollect their smiles, their encouragements, and some of the qualities that have caused our friendships to come into being in the first place. So to his dear friends at Philippi Paul was able to write, 'I thank my God every time I remember you. In all my prayers for all of you, I always pray with joy' (Phil. 1:3–4).

Paul obviously went through quite a few seasons of acute loneliness, when he felt the emotional drain of being separated from those he held dear; he shares one of those episodes with Timothy in 2 Timothy 4:9–12. At these times, rather than just pining for those far away, he would consciously bring them to mind and lift them to God in heartfelt prayer.

We often say grace before meals – but when was the last time that we gave thanks to God for our friends? Notice too that Paul was in the habit of letting people know that he was praying for them. How encouraging it is to get a note from a loved one assuring us of their prayers. Why not scribble such a note – and remember to pray too – today?

... when was the last time that we gave thanks to God for our friends?

Prayer: Lord, teach me to pray diligently and faithfully for my friends; and remind me to let them know I'm praying. Amen.